The Self-Compassion Journal

THE Self-Compassion
JOURNAL

Prompts and Practices to Inspire Kindness
in Your Thoughts, Emotions, and Actions

Alison McKleroy, MA, LMFT

ROCKRIDGE
PRESS

For general information on our other products and services, please contact our Customer Care Department within the United States at (866) 744-2665, or outside the United States at (510) 253-0500.

Paperback ISBN: 978-1-68539-642-8

Manufactured in the United States of America

Interior and Cover Designer: Stephanie Mautone
Art Producer: Maya Melenchuk
Editor: Olivia Bartz
Production Editor: Jenna Dutton
Production Manager: Martin Worthington

Author photo courtesy of Elisa Cicinelli
Illustrations © Shutterstock

10 9 8 7 6 5 4 3 2 1 0

This journal belongs to:

_____

Contents

Introduction

Hello and welcome! I'm so glad you're here.

I'm Alison, a recovering perfectionist, overachiever, and people pleaser. Like many people, I spent a lot of my life believing there was something *not enough* and *too much* about me that needed to be fixed.

My inner critic pointed out my flaws to motivate me to do better and avoid disappointing myself and others. I focused on my shortcomings, ruminated on mistakes, and pushed myself through life at volume 11 trying to find happiness and satisfaction. This approach didn't work and compounded my suffering.

If you're living with an inner critic in the background, you're in good company. The truth is that we all have a judgmental voice inside that's shaped by painful early-life experiences. Most of us have a hard time being compassionate with ourselves.

Discovering the practice of self-compassion was life-changing for me. In fact, research shows that self-compassion—treating yourself with the same kindness and understanding you would extend to a close friend or loved one—has the power to radically increase our happiness, joy, and motivation, while reducing our anxiety, stress, rumination, and depression.

With practice, I can now unhook from self-critical thoughts, bravely lean into discomfort, and accept all of my parts—rough and smooth. I can strive for excellence without beating myself up when I fall short or measuring my worth based on my achievements. I'm free to be myself and shine my light brightly.

I've spent nearly two decades as a therapist specializing in cognitive behavioral therapy, mindfulness, and art therapy, empowering people to have access to the freedom, joy, love, authenticity, creativity, and aliveness that comes when you befriend yourself.

Like any skill, self-compassion is something you can learn and build with practice. Accepting ourselves exactly as we are—even the parts we disdain—is a lifelong process. Each time you lift yourself out of a hole and back into your heart, you're strengthening this muscle.

Guided journaling is a powerful way to bring awareness to and disrupt old patterns. It offers clarity and structure for what's going on in your mind, body, heart, and soul. Journaling can release your thoughts and emotions, improve your mood, expand your perspective, and deepen your self-discovery. This journal can be a starting point to *The Self-Compassion Workbook*, or a great way to continue your journey if you've completed it.

While this journal offers an effective way to heal, any debilitating feelings of depression or anxiety may be best addressed with a medical professional. This book is not intended to replace therapy, medication, or medical treatment.

Every day you have the power, courage, and wisdom within you to transform the quality of your life and create new possibilities. Your relationship with yourself is the starting point.

Let's begin!

How to Use This Journal

This journal is packed with writing and art prompts, affirmations, and an array of exercises and step-by-step practices designed to ground yourself in self-compassion. It's organized into five sections. In section 1, you'll have an opportunity to assess where you are now and imagine where you'd like to be. Sections 2 and 3 focus on bringing self-compassion to your thoughts and emotions, while sections 4 and 5 focus on actions and integrating self-compassion into your daily life.

While many of the prompts and exercises stand alone, I recommend going through the journal in order, from start to finish, as each section builds on the previous section. That said, this is *your* journal, so if there are pages you're drawn to—or you have specific time considerations—*you do you.*

It's helpful to set a time and place to write far from distractions; this will allow space for what's inside of you to arise, and to process what you're uncovering as you work through these pages. By documenting your internal experiences, you can look back and reread what you've written to track (and celebrate!) your growth along the way.

Practice being kind to yourself and release judgments that may come up during this writing process. Growth is not linear. It takes courage to be vulnerable, discover blind spots, and sustain a new approach. You are worthy of the time, focus, and actions needed to transform your relationship with yourself.

Meeting Yourself Where You Are with Self-Compassion

If you've ever felt lost or adrift in life, you're probably familiar with how hard it can be to make any progress. Clarity helps us find focus and direction so we can take steps toward what we want for our lives. In this section you'll discover a selection of affirmations, prompts, practices, and exercises designed to empower you to get clarity on where you are and where you'd like to be. You'll have opportunities to measure your level of self-compassion, get to know your inner critic, examine your perfectionism and self-doubt, and begin to hold yourself in a kinder, more compassionate light.

Growing in self-compassion starts with seeing things as they are. Before making the changes important for healing, it's essential we get real about what's holding us back and no longer working. When you unload the weight you've been carrying, you make room for compassion.

It's freeing to create a future beyond the places we've been limiting ourselves. What we can imagine—*what could be*—is where new possibilities open and we come alive. Our dreams, visions, goals, and commitments give us direction and purpose. They inspire us into action and guide us back on our path when we inevitably get off track along the way.

Self-Compassion Assessment

Complete the following assessment (adapted from Kristin Neff's Self-Compassion Scale) to calculate your current levels of self-compassion. After you've completed this journal, you can revisit this scale to measure your growth.

Identify your response to each of the following statements in the space provided, using this scale.

ALMOST NEVER	OCCASIONALLY	SOMETIMES	FREQUENTLY	ALMOST ALWAYS
1	2	3	4	5

_____ When I fail at something important to me, I can become consumed by feelings of inadequacy.

_____ I try to be understanding toward parts of myself I don't like.

_____ When something painful happens, I try to take a balanced view.

_____ When I'm feeling down, I tend to feel others are happier than I am.

_____ I'm working on seeing my failing as part of being human.

_____ When I'm going through a hard time, I give myself the care I need.

_____ When I'm upset, I'm working on keeping my emotions in balance.

_____ I tend to feel alone in my failure.

_____ When I'm feeling down, I tend to fixate on everything that's wrong.

_____ I'm judgmental about my flaws and inadequacies.

_____ I'm intolerant of aspects of myself that I don't like.

SCORING:

_____ Total (sum of your 12 responses)

_____ Average Level (total divided by 12)

Levels of self-compassion (using your calculation from "Average Level" above):

High: 3.5 to 5 | Moderate: 2.5 to 3.5 | Low: 1 to 2.5

*I can choose to start
over, again and again,
and be kind to myself
when I get off track.*

What problem has recently been causing you significant stress and anxiety? If you were talking to an encouraging, supportive friend about it, what questions might they ask you? Write the questions, then answer them. What was it like to support yourself like a friend when you're struggling?

Notice the Difference

A key step in growing self-compassion is to examine the difference between how you treat others and how you treat yourself in difficult moments.

Think about a time when a close friend was going through a hard time. How did you respond in that situation? What did you say? How was your delivery? How did you treat your friend?

Now think about a moment when you were going through a hard time or fell short of your own expectations. How did you respond? What did you say to yourself?

Did you respond to yourself in the same way you responded to your close friend? Note any differences.

Start to consider how you might experience life differently if you were your own best friend. What would it be to like to go through a day meeting any struggles with kindness and understanding. Choose one area of your life in which your inner critical voice is having a strong, negative impact. Describe what you see as possible if you approached this area with self-compassion.

In what situations do you feel the most self-compassionate? In what scenarios is it easy to be kind, patient, and understanding toward yourself?

In what situations do you feel the least self-compassionate? What experiences trigger harsher self-criticism?

I'm worthy of kindness and compassion. I can send warmth and forgiveness in my direction.

Loving-Kindness Meditation

Loving-Kindness meditation is a practice, originating in the Buddhist tradition, to cultivate a friendly, warm-hearted attitude. You can turn this warmth toward yourself as soon as you wake up. Morning meditation is a great way to set the tone for the rest of your day.

1. Sit in a comfortable position and place your hands over your heart.

2. Take three slow, deep breaths. As you breathe, imagine your breath moving to the area of your heart.

3. Repeat to yourself the following phrases:

   a. *May I be kind to myself.*

   b. *May I accept myself just as I am.*

   c. *May I experience ease and inner peace.*

4. Take a few breaths and bask in any feeling of warmth you may experience. Bring this sensation to the rest of your day.

Inner Critic Tracking

We can become so accustomed to our self-critical voice that we don't even notice its presence. Bringing focus and awareness to this voice is the first step in loosening the grip of our inner critic's harmful thought loops that keep us stuck in self-criticism.

Over the course of five days, each time you're giving yourself a hard time, feeling disappointed with yourself or experiencing failure, write down—verbatim—what you are saying to yourself. What words or phrases do you use?

DAY 1:

_____

_____

_____

_____

DAY 2:

_____

_____

_____

_____

DAY 3:

_____

_____

_____

_____

DAY 4:

_____

_____

_____

_____

DAY 5:

_____

_____

_____

_____

Our critical inner voice takes shape early in life and often echoes the critical people in our lives, especially our caregivers. Think about the voice, language, and tone of your inner critic. Does this inner judge remind you of any person who is or was critical of you in your present or past?

The Load You Carry

Carrying around shame, guilt, and regret from the past can feel heavy. Relentlessly beating ourselves up for things we've done or failed to do can take a toll. It's difficult to get very far with a heavy load, and it can make life feel hard.

1. In the suitcase pictured, write or draw symbols for the load you've been dragging with you. What are you still blaming yourself for? What regrets are you still holding onto from the past? What mistakes are you still rehashing?

2. Imagine putting down this suitcase, opening it up, and taking some things out, releasing the load you've been dragging with you. How would it feel to lighten your load? How would you walk through the world differently? What do you need to lighten your load? What actions could you take to meet those needs?

When we wrestle with self-doubt, the cost can be huge: It keeps us playing small and missing out on opportunities for joy and fulfillment. What are some of the ways you are holding yourself back from following your dreams, passions, or interests because of self-doubt? What reasons do you give to stop yourself from moving forward in your life?

Receiving Compassion

Before you offer yourself compassion, it can be helpful to evoke what it's like to be on the receiving end of care and understanding.

1. Find a comfortable position and take a few deep breaths.

2. Close your eyes and call to mind an experience when a friend or loved one was kind and compassionate toward you in a painful moment. Recall this person's warmth, sensitivity to your suffering, and deep care for your well-being.

3. Pay attention to the sensory details. Where were you? What time of day was it? What was the person's facial expression? What did you see in their eyes? What did they say? What tone did they use?

4. How did you feel as the recipient of their care? What emotions and physical sensations can you recall?

5. Imagine this person's kindness, understanding, and compassion flowing into you. Connect with any positive emotions, such as gratitude, you may experience while reflecting on this memory of receiving care and compassion.

Warrior I Yoga Pose

Yoga is an ancient practice to promote mental and physical well-being. One of its key principles is to discover ease within effort, an excellent approach for working with self-compassion.

Warrior I Pose activates power, heart-opening stability, balance, and flexibility—a perfect pose to begin with and come back to on your self-compassion journey.

1. Begin in a standing position.

2. As you inhale, step your right foot forward and bend your knee 90 degrees. Keep your left leg straight behind you and turn your heel 45 degrees.

3. As you exhale, raise your arms overhead, torso forward, keeping your shoulders relaxed.

4. Take slow, deep breaths. Hold the position for up to one minute.

5. Repeat on the other side.

Think about an aspect of yourself you have a hard time accepting. It can be a physical characteristic, personality trait, behavior, or habit. What are the emotions and thoughts that arise when you focus on this part of you? How do you try to hide or suppress it? Are you willing to fully accept this aspect of yourself? What would it be like if you embraced this part of you?

Chasing after perfection is one of the surest ways to undermine happiness. The compulsive striving to achieve unrealistic goals results in stress, depression, and anxiety. In which areas of your life is perfectionism robbing you of joy? What is one impossible standard you're holding yourself to? How could you adjust this standard to be more realistic or stop pressuring yourself to meet it?

It's easy to confuse perfectionism with striving for excellence, but they are different. The pursuit of excellence inspires and motivates you to meet high standards without measuring your worth in terms of productivity, accomplishment, or approval from others. In which areas of your life would it make a difference to give up perfectionism to pursue excellence with enjoyment and ease? How would you feel and behave differently in each of these domains?

It takes intention and practice to give up old, unproductive patterns. The more you practice giving up what isn't working, the more easily you can free yourself from what's keeping you stuck and move forward. What are some thought or behavior patterns that are keeping you stuck or are detrimental to your well-being? Are you willing to shift these patterns? What next steps can you take?

Research shows you are 76 percent more likely to fulfill your goals when you write them down, and this number increases when you share your goals with others. In working through this journal, what are three goals or commitments you have? Who are three people in your life with whom you'd be willing to share your goals? What structures can you put in place to keep yourself accountable?

I'm not alone. Struggling is normal and part of the human experience.

Addressing Your Thoughts with Self-Compassion

Joy and suffering don't exist in our circumstances; they exist inside of us. The stories we tell ourselves–about ourselves and our circumstances–shape our mood, outlook, and behaviors.

In this section, you'll observe your thoughts with enough perspective to recognize that thoughts are just thoughts, and you don't have to automatically believe them. You'll explore the workings of your inner critic so you can break free from its spell.

As humans, we are hard-wired to be self-critical. We have a built-in system for detecting threats called a *negativity bias*, which sensitizes us to negative experiences and attunes us to our mistakes and shortcomings. Our self-critical thought patterns can become like grooves in the brain.

Thanks to the brain's neuroplasticity, however, we also have the power to rewire our minds. With practice, we can pause in a moment of suffering, unhook from thoughts, and be compassionate. This creates new pathways in the brain that shift our actions in the moment and over time. You have the freedom to choose–moment by moment–to look compassionately and honestly at your own mind and disentangle from the thoughts that keep you stuck.

Drawing Your Inner Critic

Let's get your inner critic out of your head and onto the page so you can understand it and diminish its power.

Call up your inner critic in your mind. Draw it as a character, a creature, or a cartoon. Give it a name and include speech bubbles with its common criticisms. Remember, this is not about producing a masterpiece. The creative process has transformative healing powers. Drawing is a dynamic way to bypass linear thinking, allowing us to discover something new and unexpected within ourselves.

On the following pages, you'll have a chance to dialogue with this inner critic. As you do, you can look back at this picture and let the answers emerge. The first shift needed when working with your inner critic is to stop criticizing yourself for having one and instead get curious about it. There's nothing wrong or uncommon about having an inner critic.

Ask your inner critic: What do you have to say to me? What is something you want me to know or understand? **Record what responses arise.**

Ask your inner critic: What are your biggest fears and concerns? What are you pro-tecting me from? What situations are you trying to help me avoid? **Record what responses arise.**

Ask your inner critic: What feelings or emotional risks are you protecting me from? Failure? Rejection? Embarrassment? Criticism? Shame? **Record what responses arise.**

Ask your inner critic: How are you trying to correct my behavior so I don't get into trouble, or disappoint myself or anyone else? What are you afraid would happen if you didn't play this role? Record what responses arise.

Your inner critic wants to be heard and have its intentions seen. When your inner critic is reminded that you're an adult now and can handle hard things, it's more easily freed from its main role. Write a thank-you note to your inner critic, appreciating its protection and addressing its fears and concerns. What reassurance might it need to hear?

*I can hear my inner critic
without taking its direction.
I can befriend who I
am and all my parts.*

Highest Self

When you connect to a deep wisdom within you that extends beyond the mind and its ongoing chatter, you're better equipped to break through patterns of fear, self-doubt, shame, and self-criticism. This inner wisdom and essence holds many names: *highest self, wise mind, true being, the Self, inner teacher,* or *inner guide.*

Tara Brach, renowned meditation teacher, psychologist, and author of *Radical Acceptance* and *Radical Compassion,* offers a metaphor to guide you back to your innate inner wisdom:

1. Imagine seeing a cute dog you'd like to pet—but who suddenly snarls as you approach.

2. The snarling may cause you to be scared or angry.

3. When you look more closely, however, you see one of the dog's legs is caught in a trap.

4. You may soften and feel tenderness for the dog because you understand it was snarling out of pain.

Remember this metaphor when you're in a moment of suffering: Practice stepping back and embodying your highest self. From this place, you may observe that your mind is caught in a trap. Doing this will help you offer compassion to the part of you that is in pain. With practice, it becomes easier to access this wise and compassionate part of yourself.

What do you call the awareness and wisdom that rest behind your thoughts, concerns, and fears? What is it like to experience your highest self? How do you treat yourself when you are aligned in this way?

In what ways do you connect with your highest self? During what times have you felt most connected to your highest self?

I can align with my highest self and hold myself with tenderness when my mind is caught in a trap and suffering.

Blossoms on a Brook

You can learn to hold self-critical thoughts loosely by mindfully observing your thinking. Use this meditative practice adapted from acceptance and commitment therapy (ACT) to notice your thoughts, without resisting them or assuming they're true.

1. Close your eyes. Take slow breaths.

2. Visualize sitting at the edge of a gently flowing brook with flower blossoms floating along the surface. Take in the scene: time of day, sounds, colors, smells, etc.

3. Take each thought that enters your mind and imagine placing it on a blossom.

4. Allow the blossom to float downstream.

5. Repeat this with each thought.

6. Allow the brook to flow at its own pace.

7. If a thought such as *I'm not doing this right* arises, put that thought on a blossom, too.

In the Blossoms on a Brook practice, which thoughts were easy to let drift downstream? Which thoughts got stuck, eddied, or came back again? Write any reflections you have.

My thoughts are just thoughts. I can observe and allow my thoughts to drift downstream like blossoms on a brook.

I'm Having the Thought . . .

Here is another method from ACT to use when you're accepting self-critical thoughts as facts. With a little space from your thoughts, you can see them for what they are: just thoughts.

1. Think about a time when you were upset with yourself. Write down one self-critical thought.

   Example: *I'm always falling short.*

2. Rewrite that thought by preceding it with *I'm having the thought that . . .*

   Example: *I'm having the thought that I'm always falling short.*

3. For more distance, rewrite the previous thought, adding *I notice I'm having the thought that . . .*

Example: *I notice I'm having the thought that I'm always falling short.*

Did your perception shift? Are you willing to consider that your thought might not be true? Write down your reflections.

Unhooking from Self-Critical Beliefs

Let's look at a few more ACT techniques to help you get unhooked and not take your thoughts too seriously. By inviting play, you allow the belief's meaning or significance to drop away.

Choose one self-critical belief and practice each technique for at least thirty seconds or until it loses some of its meaning. Repeat with others from the list that resonate.

- I'm defective.
- I'm incompetent.
- I'm unlovable.
- I'm worthless.
- I'm weak.
- I'm too sensitive.

- I'm too emotional.
- I'm inferior.
- I'm damaged.
- I'm a fraud.
- I'm a burden.
- I'm bad.

1. Say it *very* slowly in your head.

2. Repeat it *very* quickly.

3. Sing it to the tune of "Happy Birthday."

Cognitive Restructuring

In cognitive behavioral therapy (CBT), *cognitive restructuring* is a process used to challenge unhelpful thoughts and replace them with more accurate, balanced ones.

1. Write a self-defeating belief.

   Example: *I'm a failure.*

2. Connect with your common humanity and accept it.

   Example: *Like all humans, I've had a lot of failures and will continue to.*

3. Dispute it.

   Example: *I haven't failed at everything and have had successes, too.*

4. What can you do?

Example: *I can learn and grow from my failures.*

_____

_____

_____

5. Combine these elements to create a replacement thought.

Example: *Like all humans, I've had a lot of failures and will continue to. I haven't failed at everything and have had successes, too. I can learn and grow from them.*

_____

_____

_____

It's easy to become identified with the incessant stream of thinking in our minds. What is it like to shift from listening to the content of your mind to being the awareness in the background? How often do you experience this shift throughout your day? What helps you make this shift?

As you sharpen your focus on listening to the voice in your head, what repetitive thought patterns are you noticing? What old records are playing in your head? How long have these thought patterns been going on? What has been the impact of these repetitive thought patterns on the different areas of your life?

Identifying Thinking Errors

In CBT, identifying your *thinking errors* is another way to help you untwist self-defeating thinking.

Following are four common thinking errors adapted from the work of CBT pioneers Aaron Beck and David Burns. Complete the chart with two of your own negative thoughts.

Should-ing: Imposing unrealistic expectations on yourself.
Filtering: Focusing on only the negative aspects.
Mind Reading: Believing you know what people are thinking.
Unrealistic Comparing: Comparing yourself unfavorably to others.

SELF-DEFEATING THOUGHT	THINKING ERROR	COMPASSIONATE REPLACEMENT
I shouldn't be so self-conscious.	Should-ing	*Everyone feels self-conscious sometimes.*
I ruined the date.	Filtering	*It's natural to feel nervous. I can try again.*
Everyone thought I was incompetent.	Mind Reading	*I can't read people's minds.*
I don't have as many friends as she does.	Unrealistic Comparing	*I'm on my own journey on my own timeline.*

What would it look like to go through your day with the ability to loosen the grip of self-critical thoughts? If you weren't automatically believing your thoughts are the truth, what do you see as possible for yourself and your life? What next steps can you take?

Embracing Your Emotions with Self-Compassion

Stop being so anxious! When you criticize yourself in this way, you may be trying to squash your feelings and make them go away. You've probably noticed this doesn't work. Let's look at a metaphor from acceptance and commitment therapy (ACT) that illustrates this self-defeating process.

What if trying to control your feelings is like trying to push an inflated beach ball underwater? Each time you try to push the ball underwater, it pops back up. It takes all your strength to keep it underwater. Struggling with it in this way is not only futile, but also exhausting. What if you could stop wasting your energy on an impossible task and just take the ball back to your beach towel? In that case, you'd be able to use your arms to enjoy a swim!

Emotions can be challenging. This section is designed to empower you to better understand and embrace your emotions and grow your capacity to be present with your pain so you're free to *enjoy your swim.*

When you try to ignore, avoid, or get rid of your emotions, or criticize yourself for having them, you reinforce where you are stuck and limit your freedom. It takes bravery to turn toward and lean into painful inner experiences. This section offers you opportunities to bring curiosity and kindness to your suffering so you can meet each moment with greater wisdom, courage, and compassion.

Let's start with an emotional check-in. How are you feeling right now? Write or draw any emotions or bodily sensations you're experiencing. What are some feelings you've been experiencing lately? What recent situations have produced distressing feelings?

What feelings do you want to experience more of in your life? What recent situations have produced joyful feelings? What recent situations have produced feelings of happiness or contentment? When was the last time you felt completely relaxed or at ease?

Heart Map

Artmaking empowers us to express emotions by taking what's inside and making it visible. Creating art can also be a powerful form of self-care. You can use this exercise when you're having a difficult moment, or as a daily check-in.

What feelings are in your heart? Use the legend to write each feeling and select a different color to represent each one. Now color in sections of the heart to represent how much of each feeling you're experiencing.

When you look at your Heart Map, what do you notice? Did anything surprise you about how the heart or legend was filled or divided? What was it like to do this exercise? What are ways you check in with how you're feeling?

The way we handle emotions is often modeled by how our caregivers dealt with them our childhoods. As a child, what feelings were you taught not to feel or express? What feelings were encouraged? What feelings were discouraged? How were distressing feelings handled by your caregivers?

As an adult, how do you handle emotions? How has your life been shaped by the way emotions were handled by caregivers during childhood? What feelings are distressing for you to feel or express now? What do you need to allow yourself to feel and express them? What do you fear might happen?

Your inner critic may blame or judge you for your emotional reactions. This can add more suffering to the pain you're experiencing. Becoming curious and allowing yourself to fully experience your feelings is a powerful skill. Choose one emotion you find difficult to accept. What feels uncomfortable about this feeling that might keep you from accepting it?

I can let my heart alchemize painful emotions. I can choose to feel my feelings, even uncomfortable ones.

Permission Slip

Our inner critic holds us to unrealistic standards when it comes to our very human emotions. It might restrain you so you don't lose control, experience judgment, get overwhelmed, or lash out. It's normal to fear what might happen if you allowed yourself to feel the full range of your emotions. You can start by giving yourself permission to *feel your feelings* rather than criticize yourself for them.

Fill out the following slips using feelings that you often resist or avoid experiencing.

PERMISSION SLIP

I, _____, give myself permission to feel _____.

It's okay to feel this way; it's part of the human experience.

Signature: _____   Date: _____

PERMISSION SLIP

I, _____, give myself permission to feel _____.

It's okay to feel this way; it's part of the human experience.

Signature: _____   Date: _____

PERMISSION SLIP

I, _____, give myself permission to feel _____.

It's okay to feel this way; it's part of the human experience.

Signature: _____   Date: _____

How did it feel to write yourself a permission slip? Was there anything holding you back? Were some feelings easier than others to give yourself permission to feel?

Riding the 90-Second Wave

The *amygdala* is a part of the brain that's responsible for our reactions to perceived danger, referred to as the *fight, flight or freeze* response. When it's activated, we often act without thinking. Our amygdala can get "hijacked" easily since it can't differentiate between a tiger chasing you and a stressful email.

According to neuroscientist Jill Bolte Taylor, it takes only ninety seconds to ride out a feeling. When you pause to identify your emotion, label it and allow it to move through you and dissipate, this calms activity in the amygdala and flushes out the chemicals that put you on high alert. Any remaining emotional response is due to negative thoughts that are re-stimulating the physiological reaction, keeping you in an emotional loop. Let's practice.

1. Identify your emotional reaction:

    a. What's going on in your body? (Example: fast heartbeat, sweating, chest tightness)

    b. What's going on in your mind? (Example: harsh judgments, racing thoughts)

3. Label your emotion without judgment. (Example: *I'm feeling ashamed*; *Anger is here*)

4. Ride the wave of emotion for ninety seconds. Let it rise, crest, and fall without trying to change it.

When we're in distress, instead of welcoming our inner experiences, we may feel like we need to actively control them. What are some ways you try to fix, control, or stay positive when you're experiencing suffering?

It's natural to try to avoid discomfort and pain. This brings short-term relief but keeps us stuck in the long term. In what ways do you avoid being with uncomfortable feelings? What activities do you engage in to distract yourself?

When we're experiencing a challenging emotional experience, it can be easy to bottle up our feelings, or push them aside, to get on with our day. Over time, this bottling can lead to burnout. In what ways do you bottle up your feelings? What has been the impact of bottling up your emotions over time? What outlets can you use to express these emotions?

Hands on Your Heart

We are wired for touch. Research has found that humans have a "care circuit." Physical touch activates the parasympathetic nervous system, which helps us feel calm and safe, and releases oxytocin, a hormone that produces feelings of love, security, and connection. Giving yourself soothing touch is a simple way to comfort yourself.

1. When you notice distressing emotions, take one deep breath.

2. Place your hands over your heart.

3. Feel the weight of your hands on your chest.

4. Take three slow, deep breaths into the space around your heart.

5. You can gently rub, tap, or intertwine your fingers.

6. Acknowledge this simple act of tenderness.

I can put my hands on my heart and bravely lean into discomfort. I can ride the waves of my emotions.

Emotions as Messengers

One way to cultivate curiosity about and compassion for our emotions is to first acknowledge the gifts they offer us. In every situation, our feelings point to our needs and values underneath. They show us what matters and deepen our self-acceptance.

In this exercise, adapted from David Burns's book *Feeling Great*, we'll reframe emotions through a positive lens. In the left column, write five feelings you've experienced in the last week. In the right column, write what each feeling might show that's important to you for each situation.

Example:

EMOTIONS	WHAT'S IMPORTANT TO ME
Resentful	I value acknowledgment and appreciation.
Angry	I value respect and consideration.
Anxious	I care about safety and protection.
Ashamed	I have high standards for myself and want to belong.
Lonely	I value connection.
Sad	I care deeply about someone or something.

Now write your own:

EMOTIONS	WHAT'S IMPORTANT TO ME

What would you say to a friend who is struggling with their emotions? What feelings would a friend have permission to feel? What encouraging words and tone would you use? Is this different from how you treat yourself? If yes, how? Note the differences.

Self-Empathy

Self-empathy is part of a process used in nonviolent communication (NVC) to help you get in touch with your feelings and needs when you're in a challenging situation with others. You ask yourself three questions: *What am I observing? What feelings are arising from this situation? What unmet needs do I have that are the root cause of my feelings?* By answering these questions, you begin to create inner peace.

1. *What am I observing?* Describe it in a neutral way, as if watching through a video camera.

   (Example: *When I see* ... my partner scrolling on his phone while I'm talking to him ...)

   When I hear/see ...

2. What feelings are arising?

   (Example: ... *I feel* annoyed and hurt)

   I feel ...

3. What am I needing?

   (Example: ... *because I need consideration and to be heard*)

   Because I need ...

What are some other unmet needs underneath your distressing feelings? What are the needs or values underneath your anger? Your frustration? Your hurt? Your loneliness? Your resentment?

Postcard to Your Future Self

Do you remember how good it feels to go to your mailbox and discover a postcard from a friend? You're going to write a letter to your future self who will get to experience those positive feelings when you need it most.

Write a letter to yourself to read when you're having a hard time, feeling down, or experiencing painful emotions. What wise, compassionate words would feel comforting and reassuring to receive? What reminders of common humanity would be helpful to hear? Write those friendly phrases to your future self. You can come back to this page when you need to hear this message in the future.

It's okay to feel the way I feel. My emotions point to what's important to me. May I be kind to myself.

Putting Self-Compassion into Action

Turned inward, *compassion* is noticing our own suffering with a desire to alleviate it. Kristin Neff, a pioneering researcher in the field of self-compassion, says the essential question of self-compassion is simply this: "What do I need right now?" In this section, you'll explore what actions you can take to understand and meet your own needs.

Our inner critic can keep reminding us how we could have done something better or push us to strive harder. Research shows that a self-compassionate response to our shortcomings is more effective at motivating us to take responsibility for past mistakes, set new goals after failure, and engage in habits that promote well-being.

You can use many different strategies to take care of yourself. Sometimes the situation may call for comforting actions, such as drawing yourself a bath when you're upset. Other times, you might take courageous action, such as saying no to a request, to protect your needs.

In this section, you're empowered to release guilt and shame and learn from your actions when they weren't aligned with your values.

Self-Forgiveness

When we're feeling guilt or shame about past events, forgiving ourselves can feel impossible. But it's a powerful choice we can make to free ourselves from the past. Self-forgiveness is not condoning your behavior or taking yourself off the hook. It's showing yourself grace when you've done something that wasn't aligned with your values and trusting you can learn from the experience. You can't change what happened in the past, but you can change how it impacts you in the present and future.

Choose a decision or action you're having difficulty forgiving yourself for and complete this exercise:

1. When I think about this situation, I feel . . . _____

2. These feelings show that I value . . . _____

3. I can accept full responsibility for my actions and any harm that was caused. I also recognize that all humans are complex and make mistakes. What makes me human is . . . _____

4. Learning from mistakes is how I grow. This mistake has taught me . . . _____

5. I can try a new approach next time. Next time I will . . . _____

6. Rewrite the message on page 79 as is, or in your own words.

I'm willing to offer myself grace. I can trust myself to learn and grow from this. I can choose to forgive myself and allow myself the chance to start over.

What are some other actions or situations you could forgive yourself for? Have you been punishing yourself or rehashing what happened? If yes, how? Are you willing to forgive yourself? What would it look like to offer yourself grace and understanding in these situations?

Reframing Failure

Failure simply means a lack of success or not meeting an expectation. Self-compassionate people offer themselves the grace to fail, learn what there is to learn, and bounce back more quickly with a willingness to risk trying again. By reflecting on your failures in a way that's constructive, you can gain insight and transform your future.

List four significant personal and/or professional failures you've experienced in your life and examine what you've learned from them.

Summarize what happened, note what you learned, and write what you would do differently next time.

	FAILURE	LESSONS LEARNED	NEXT TIME, I WOULD . . .
1.			
2.			
3.			
4.			

What possibilities become available to you when you reframe your failures? What new opportunities could you risk taking if you weren't afraid of failing?

I'm more than the sum of my mistakes. It's human to fail and make mistakes. I'm learning and growing.

Saying No to Requests

A lot of people say yes because they're afraid to disappoint others or lose relationships. Saying no is a courageous expression of our self-compassion; it protects our finite time and energy.

When considering a request, ask yourself:

1. *Does it light me up?*

2. *Can I fulfill this commitment with the time and resources needed in a way that meets my standard for excellence?*

3. *Am I saying yes because I want to and not just to avoid the discomfort of disappointing someone?*

If your response is *yes*, go for it!

If your response is *no*, remind yourself that a no to someone else is a yes to you. Your needs matter. It's okay to prioritize your inner peace.

Suggestions for saying no:

I appreciate you considering me. I've got other commitments at this time.

I can't make it, but thanks for thinking of me.

In what ways do you struggle with boundaries? In what areas in your life do you see that setting boundaries in your relationships could protect your well-being? What steps could you take?

Do you automatically say yes or spread yourself too thin? In what ways do you abandon or push aside your own needs? If so, what's the impact on you, your life, your work, and your relationships?

What challenging conversations are you avoiding or hesitant to initiate? What are you afraid might happen? What is something you've been wanting to tell a friend, partner, family member, or colleague? What support do you need to empower you to use your voice and bring it up?

Sometimes we feel scared, guilty, confused, or regretful after we've set a boundary. Just because we feel uncomfortable doesn't mean we've made a mistake. How could you handle the pain or discomfort that might come from saying no or maintaining your boundaries with someone? How could you soothe yourself in the face of distress?

Filling Your Cup

Sometimes our inner critic tells us that meeting our needs is selfish or self-indulgent, so we may ignore our needs. Just as you might offer a cup of tea or say "Let's take a walk" to a friend in distress, you can practice recognizing and prioritizing your own needs with the same warmth and care.

You can't pour from an empty cup. When you take the actions needed to support your own well-being, you are filling your cup so you can show up as your best self.

WHAT ACTIVITIES FILL MY CUP?

1. _____
2. _____
3. _____
4. _____
5. _____

WHAT ACTIVITIES DRAIN MY CUP?

1. _____
2. _____
3. _____
4. _____
5. _____

Take a moment to assess your cup. How full is it right now? How can you tell? What does it feel like to go through your day with this level?

What are some signs that indicate your cup is nearly empty or empty? What can you do to support your well-being when you sense your cup is getting low?

You're worthy of your cup being full. What are some signs that indicate your cup is full? When was the last time your cup was full? How do you experience your life when your cup is full? What steps could you take to ensure your cup is full?

Sensory Self-Soothing Kit

When we're distressed or overwhelmed, it's helpful to have a kit on hand with things that offer soothing and calm. The more we learn to soothe ourselves in hard times, the easier it gets.

Customize a kit by filling a box with items that reflect your needs and preferences. Consider your available senses and what brings comfort for each one.

Some ideas to build your own kit include:

- Vision: photos, affirmations, positive notes, journal and pen, coloring book and pencils

- Touch: stones or crystals, stress ball, fidget, lotion, eye mask, soft socks, blanket

- Sound: music playlist, headphones, bell, sound app

- Taste: tea, mint, favorite snack

- Smell: aromatherapy oils, candle, scented lotion, dried lavender

Glossary of Needs

Almost everything we do is to meet a need. Our emotions show us when needs are met or unmet. Being clear about our needs and taking action to meet them improves our well-being, both in the moment and over the course of our lives.

Using the following list, choose one need and brainstorm strategies you can use to meet it. Focus on this need for a day or a week. Repeat the process for other needs.

GLOSSARY OF NEEDS

Acceptance	Connection	Intimacy
Affection	Consideration	Joy
Appreciation/ Acknowledgment	Contribution	Justice
	Creativity	Kindness
Authenticity	Ease	Love
Autonomy	Equality	Movement
Be heard	Freedom	Order
Be seen	Fun and play	Peace
Beauty	Growth and learning	Reliability
Celebration	Harmony	Respect
Clarity	Honesty	Rest
Comfort	Inclusion	Safety
Community	Inspiration	Trust
Compassion	Intentions seen	Understanding

What do you consider some of your most important needs? How do you meet them? What gets in the way of meeting them? What would it be like if you were routinely meeting these needs? What steps could you take to regularly meet your most important needs?

_____

_____

_____

_____

_____

_____

_____

_____

_____

_____

_____

_____

_____

_____

_____

_____

I'm worthy of prioritizing my own needs. When my cup is full, I have more to pour from—for myself and others.

Celebrating the Victories

Perfectionism can leave you so future-oriented that it blinds you to your incremental progress and victories. Taking stock of your accomplishments and acknowledging progress not only reduces stress and burnout, it also inspires you to keep going. Most important, celebrating your wins allows you to enjoy yourself along the way.

Write your personal and/or professional wins (small, large, or huge) in the medals pictured. Take a moment to deeply appreciate the effort, skill, and courage it took for each accomplishment.

In reviewing your wins, what feelings come up? Other ways to acknowledge accomplishments are by noting them in a "good news" file; sharing these moments with friends, family, or colleagues; or writing them down in a journal to track them. What steps could you take to track and acknowledge your successes and achievements more frequently?

I'm not perfect and I don't have to be. I'm a human on my own journey and I can celebrate my wins along the way.

Practicing Self-Compassion Every Day

Shifting habitual patterns requires awareness, intention, and practice. It may feel like nothing's changing, but slowly and surely, your life is transforming. Self-compassion is not a quick fix. It's a lifelong practice that deepens over time. In this section, you'll reflect on what you've learned about yourself throughout these pages and integrate the practices that are most helpful in your daily life. You'll explore ways to maintain your well-being through mindfulness, self-care, and gratitude in your day-to-day life.

Our daily life provides boundless opportunities for self-compassion practice. It's easy to move through each day on autopilot. But when you practice bringing awareness to your patterns, you can step back, observe, and choose a new way to relate to yourself and face your difficulties. At any moment you can connect with your highest self, along with the wisdom and compassion that is already within you.

Every day you're presented with new opportunities to get back up, brush yourself off, and keep loving yourself *just the way you are*.

What are you learning about yourself as you work through this journal? What changes are you noticing? How have you grown since the first pages of this journal?

Your Self-Compassion Plan

Growing your self-compassion and sustaining your well-being require that you make positive changes. Wendy Wood, author of *Good Habits, Bad Habits*, suggests you choose behaviors that are easy and immediately rewarding, and do them repeatedly. She also notes it takes two to three months to make a habit automatic.

Review your journal and choose what you want to integrate into your day-to-day.

Name of exercise/practice: _____   Page number: _____

It was helpful because . . . _____

_____

_____

_____

I can integrate it by: _____

_____

_____

_____

Name of exercise/practice: _____   Page number: _____

It was helpful because . . . _____

_____

_____

_____

I can integrate it by: _____

_____

_____

_____

Name of exercise/practice: _____ Page number: _____

It was helpful because . . . _____

_____

_____

_____

I can integrate it by: _____

_____

_____

In reviewing your work in this journal, which parts have been challenging? Which parts have been satisfying? Which parts have been the most helpful? What were you surprised by? What wisdom do you want to take with you? What are your biggest take-aways?

Box of Affirmations

Using self-compassionate affirmations helps break our self-critical thinking habits. They are most effective when they are practiced daily and reinforced with visual reminders. They can be repeated any time, any place, and with enough repetition, they can become automatic.

Make your own box to hold your favorite affirmations, and write some affirmation index cards.

1. Use wrapping paper or magazine images to glue inspirational visuals or messages to the outside of a tissue box. Choose colors that bring you joy.

2. Flip through this journal and make a list of affirmations that resonate with you, and/or write your own. Keep them simple, construct them in the present tense, and avoid using negative words.

3. Copy your affirmations onto index cards, add any embellishments, then place them into your box. Pull one or two cards to focus on for the day or the week, or place them in your environment as reminders.

Morning and Evening Rituals

A routine is a sequence of actions, but a ritual is a meaningful practice that has a sense of purpose. Experiment with these prompts as part of a daily ritual. Bookending your day with intention and reflection can improve your mood and change the course of your life.

MORNING CHECK-IN:

My focus for today is . . .

I can meet my needs by . . .

Body:

Mind:

Heart:

Soul:

I'm grateful for . . .

My positive affirmation is . . .

EVENING CHECK-IN:

One word to describe my day is . . .

My challenges were . . .

What I learned . . .

What went well . . .

I can let go of . . .

Three things I'm grateful for are . . . _____ , _____ , _____

How do you want to feel at the start of your day? What small or big shifts could you make to your morning routine to support this feeling? How could you bring more intention to your mornings?

How do you want to feel at the end of your day? What small or big shifts could you make to your evening routine to support this feeling? How could you bring more reflection to your evening?

"Taking and Giving" Meditation

The "taking and giving" meditation, called *tonglen,* is an ancient Tibetan Buddhist practice to cultivate compassion in which you breathe in suffering and breathe out compassion. Tonglen can be done as a formal practice or used on the spot when you're experiencing pain.

1. Sit in a comfortable position, close your eyes, and take some deep breaths.

2. As you inhale, picture a dark cloud of smoke and imagine you're breathing in pain and suffering—yours and that of the people around the world who are experiencing the same.

3. Imagine transforming this darkness inside you into radiant light. As you exhale, imagine sending out the light of compassion and well-being to yourself and everyone who needs it.

May I be happy. May I be peaceful. May all beings be free from suffering.

Self-Appreciation

Appreciating yourself can feel a little awkward or uncomfortable at first. When you practice self-appreciation each day, you're creating new neural patterns and reinforcing self-compassion. In moments of self-judgment, this makes it easier to remember and hold the larger context of who you are—embracing both the dark parts and the light parts.

Fill in the blanks that follow. You can revisit and add to this page each day.

What I value about myself is . . .

Three qualities I appreciate about myself are . . .

What my friends would say they appreciate about me is . . .

What my family or loved ones would say they appreciate about me is . . .

My ten biggest strengths are . . .

The three best compliments I've received are . . .

I'm most proud of . . .

What was it like for you to appreciate yourself? What feelings came up? When was the last time you paused to give yourself credit for how far you've come or how much you've grown? How could you integrate self-appreciation into your daily life?

*Like everyone in the world,
I have both strengths
and weaknesses. I am
a work in progress.*

Yin Yoga Poses

One teaching of the yoga tradition is to seek balance between effort and ease. Yin yoga poses are intended to downregulate the nervous system, relieve stress and tension, lower anxiety and deepen relaxation. The yin poses give you permission to slow down, let go, and turn inward. They are great to do when you're needing calm, rest, or a sense of peace.

Hold each pose for two to three minutes, while paying attention to your breath and allowing any physical sensations that arise.

Viparita Karani (Legs-up-the-wall pose)   *Balasana* (Child's pose)

Savasana (Corpse pose)

My needs matter and I can choose to care for myself. I am worthy of rest and play.

What are your favorite ways to slow down, rest, and restore your energy? How can you incorporate these activities into your daily life?

What physical self-care activities do you enjoy? How do you meet your need for movement? How do you meet your need for fun and play? How do you meet your need for rest?

What emotional self-care activities do you enjoy? How do you meet your need to be heard and understood? How do you meet your need for joy? How do you meet your need for comfort and inner harmony?

What mental self-care activities do you enjoy? How do you meet your need for peace and calm? How do you meet your need for stimulation? How do you meet your need for learning and growth?

What social self-care activities do you enjoy? How do you meet your need for love and connection? How do you meet your need for community? How do you meet your need for fun and play with others?

What creative self-care activities do you enjoy? How do you meet your need for imagination and flow? What creative activities did you enjoy most as a child? Which creative activities bring you the most enjoyment as an adult? When was the last time you did a creative activity? How can you best support your creativity?

I give myself permission to rest, take breaks, and enjoy my life. I'm learning to be my own best friend.

Thirty Days of Self-Care

When you create and follow a plan for your self-care, it takes the guesswork out of what to do each day. This reduces decision-making fatigue, which is a big obstacle to forming positive habits.

Fill in the calendar with self-care ideas from the list or create your own. Each day is a chance to start again.

SELF-CARE IDEAS

Go outside	Call someone I love	Dance to music
Stay off social media	Watch a sunset	Go to bed early
Watch my favorite movie	Take a bath	Make my favorite meal
Meditate	Spend time in nature	Listen to a new podcast
Do yoga	Write in my journal	Have coffee with a friend
Take a walk	Read my favorite book	Plan a fun weekend
Stay in my pajamas	Take a nap	
Listen to music	Do a creative activity	

1	2	3	4	5
6	7	8	9	10
11	12	13	14	15
16	17	18	19	20
21	22	23	24	25
26	27	28	29	30

A Final Note

Congratulations! This is a great moment to stop and acknowledge all of your work. It takes time, intention, and commitment to keep showing up for yourself, deepening your self-discovery, and filling these pages.

Self-compassion is an ongoing practice. The goal isn't to get rid of something within ourselves, throw out our "bad" parts, or push ourselves into a better version, but to keep practicing being a great friend to ourselves—exactly as we are—every day.

Self-critical thoughts and challenging emotions are part of the human experience and as such, they will never go away. We have a choice in how we respond to them, however. We can pause and catch ourselves in a self-defeating spiral and unhook from our thoughts. We can notice a painful emotion and lean into the discomfort. We can forgive and trust ourselves to learn from our mistakes and failures. And we can always connect with our highest self—the part of us that is infinitely wise, aware, and compassionate. The more we practice fully accepting ourselves, the brighter we radiate our light into the world.

At peace with yourself and anchored in your greatness, you're more open to the endless possibilities to experience joy and the freedom to be yourself, take risks, and play big in life. May the rest of your journey continue with courage, kindness, and the warm glow of compassion.

Resources

BOOKS

Beautiful You: A Daily Guide to Radical Self-Acceptance by Rosie Molinary

Molinary is an educator and activist. This book offers daily actions to encourage women to love themselves, break habits of self-criticism, and embrace a healthy self-image.

Nonviolent Communication: A Language of Life by Marshall Rosenberg

Dr. Rosenberg was a psychologist and teacher who developed a process for self-empathy and resolving conflicts with others with empathy.

Radical Compassion: Learning to Love Yourself and Your World with the Practice of RAIN by Tara Brach

Dr. Brach is a world-renowned meditation teacher and psychologist whose teachings focus on cultivating compassion. This is a practical book with a focus on the meditation practice called *RAIN* (**R**ecognize, **A**llow, **I**nvestigate, **N**urture).

Set Boundaries, Find Peace: A Guide to Reclaiming Yourself by Nedra Tawwab

Tawwab is a psychotherapist with a focus on boundaries and relationships. This book helps us cultivate healthy boundaries and speak up for what we need.

The Body is Not an Apology: The Power of Radical Self-Love by Sonya Renee Taylor

Taylor is a poet, educator, and activist who invites readers to counteract indoctrinated body shame, celebrate strength, and awaken self-love.

The Gifts of Imperfection by Brené Brown

Dr. Brown is a research professor who has spent twenty years studying courage, vulnerability, shame, and empathy. Her book is a guide for releasing the quest for perfection and embracing authenticity.

The Wisdom of No Escape: And the Path of Loving-Kindness by Pema Chödrön

Chödrön is a world-renowned Buddhist teacher. This book is a guide for how to stop running from our pain, trust our basic goodness, and embrace life just the way it is.

WEBSITES

Self-Compassion.org

This excellent website, curated by Dr. Kristin Neff, is filled with many resources to practice self-compassion, including assessment tools, meditations, exercises, and links to her books.

References

Beck, Aaron T. *Cognitive Therapy and Emotional Disorders*. New York: International Universities Press, 1976.

Brach, Tara. "Feeling Overwhelmed? Remember RAIN: Four Steps to Stop Being So Hard on Ourselves." Mindful. February 7, 2019. mindful.org/tara-brach-rain -mindfulness-practice.

Burns, David. *Feeling Great: The Revolutionary New Treatment for Depression and Anxiety*. Eau Claire, WI: Pesi Publishing and Media, 2020.

Chen, Serena. "Give Yourself a Break: The Power of Self-Compassion." *Harvard Business Review*, October 2018. hbr.org/2018/09/give-yourself-a-break-the-power -of-self-compassion.

Chödrön, Pema. "How to Practice Tonglen." Lion's Roar. January 14, 2022. lionsroar .com/how-to-practice-tonglen.

———. "Meditation is the Key to Knowing Yourself." Lion's Roar. January 13, 2021. lionsroar.com/the-key-to-knowing-ourselves.

David, Susan. *Emotional Agility: Get Unstuck, Embrace Change and Thrive in Work and Life*. New York: Penguin Random House, 2016.

Harris, Russ. *The Happiness Trap: How To Stop Struggling and Start Living*. Boston: Trumpeter, 2008.

Johnson, Joy. *The Self-Compassion Workbook*. Emeryville, CA: Rockridge Press, 2020.

Neff, Kristin. *Fierce Self-Compassion: How Women Can Harness Kindness to Speak Up, Claim Their Power, and Thrive.* New York: Harper Wave, 2021.

Neff, Kristin, and Christopher Germer. *The Mindful Self-Compassion Workbook: A Proven Way to Accept Yourself, Build Inner Strength, and Thrive.* New York: Guilford Press, 2018.

Raes, Filip, Elizabeth Pommier, Kirstin D. Neff, and Dinska Van Gucht. "Construction and Factorial Validation of a Short Form of the Self-Compassion Scale." *Clinical Psychology & Psychotherapy* 18 (May 2011), 250–255. doi.org/10.1002/cpp.702.

Rosenberg, Marshall. *Nonviolent Communication: A Language of Life.* Encinitas, CA: PuddleDancer Press, 2003.

Shwartz, Richard. *No Bad Parts: Healing Trauma and Restoring Wholeness with the Internal Family Systems Model.* Louisville, CO: Sounds True, 2001.

Taylor, Jill Bolte. *Whole Brain Living: The Anatomy of Choice and the Four Characters That Drive Our Life.* New York: Hay House, Inc., 2021.

Wood, Wendy. *Good Habits, Bad Habits: The Science of Making Positive Changes That Stick.* New York: Farrar, Straus and Giroux: 2019.

Acknowledgments

I want to wholeheartedly thank and appreciate:

My husband, Neil, for his unwavering love, support, and encouragement.

My children, L and S, for the joy they bring me.

My parents, Alex and Kaye McKleroy, and my family, for their support.

Pattie and Samantha Fitzsimmons, for their care.

All my dear friends for their steadfast support. A special thank you to Serena Naramore, Melissa Schilling, and Jennie Powe Runde for their weekly encouragement.

My editors, Olivia Bartz and Aric Dutelle, and my team at Rockridge Press for their skilled attention.

The leaders who've guided me: Pema Chödrön, Tara Brach, Kirstin Neff, Christopher Germer, Sharon Salzberg, Brené Brown, Stephen Hayes, Russ Harris, David Burns, Aaron Beck, Marshall Rosenberg, Thich Nhat Hanh, Ram Dass, the Dalai Lama, and Richard Schwartz.

About the Author

Alison McKleroy, MA, LMFT, is a cognitive behavioral therapist and art therapist, coach, author, speaker, and artist. She is the founder of Center for Spark®, offering coaching courses and workshops to empower people to light up the world with their joy, aliveness, and unique spark. Drawing on nearly two decades of clinical experience and training, Alison enjoys adapting insights from psychology, neuroscience, art therapy, mindfulness, and Eastern traditions into tools for joyful living.

Her work is featured in a variety of publications, including Verywell Mind, PsychCentral, and Medical News Today. She enjoys life with her husband and two children, and their adventures in the world.

Find out more at CenterForSpark.com.